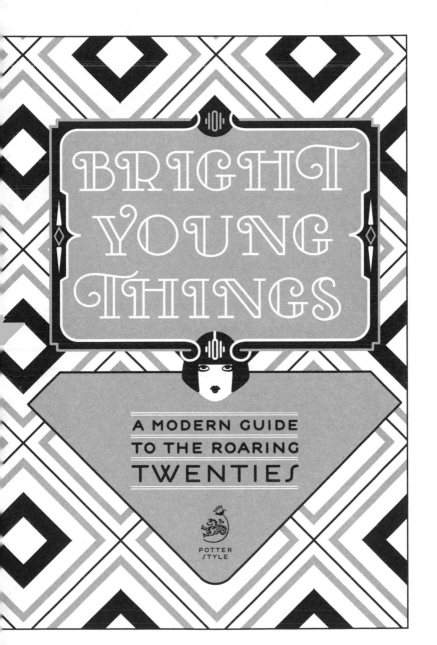

BRIGHT YOUNG THINGS

A MODERN GUIDE TO THE ROARING TWENTIES

POTTER
STYLE

ALISON MALONEY

THE PARTIES WERE BIGGER.

THE PACE WAS FASTER,

THE SHOWS

WERE BROADER,

THE BUILDINGS

WERE HIGHER,

the morals were looser, **AND THE LIQUOR** WAS CHEAPER.

—*F. Scott Fitzgerald on the 1920s in* THE GREAT GATSBY

CONTENTS

ENTERTAIN YOURSELF

ENTERTAINMENT AND GLAMOUR ◆ 112

WELCOME,
YOU BRIGHT YOUNG THING

Being a Bright Young Thing means viewing life as one long party. Consider this book your cordial invitation.

The Roaring Twenties was an era of clinking glasses, clattering automobiles, and big, brassy jazz tunes. Flappers—donning low-cut necklines and close-cropped bobs—smoked cigarettes and sipped cocktails out of porcelain tea cups in clandestine speakeasies. It was the time of the Charleston, when debutantes and princes shared dance floors with gangsters and drug dealers . . . and everyone danced all night.

Bright Young Things (as the youth culture was called) rebelled against the stuffy old-world views of their parents and paved the way for modern society, influencing everything from music and social scenes to fashion trends and evolving gender roles. They partied and lived life with no-holds-barred passion, and their joie de vivre became legendary.

So come on in, make yourself a drinkie-poo, and take a few pointers from the pioneers of cool.

THE BRIGHT
YOUNG STATE
OF MIND

IF IT'S NAUGHTY TO ROUGE YOUR LIPS,

SHAKE YOUR SHOULDERS

AND SHAKE YOUR HIPS, THEN the ANSWER IS, "I WANNA BE BAD!"

—*Buddy DeSylva*, "I WANT TO BE BAD"

THE POSTWAR PARTY

W ith World War I consigned to history—and the decline of the aristocracy as yet a distant threat—the twenties were a golden age. The previous decade had been dominated by war, with men from all walks of life fighting and dying on the battlefields of Europe, while women filled the soldiers' shoes in the workplace and gained a newfound independence as a result. As the 1920s dawned, a new generation, who had lost older brothers and fathers but who had escaped the conflict themselves, were becoming adults.

The shackles of wartime gave way to the euphoria of peacetime freedom, and the sadness of loss made the young survivors all the more determined to live life to the fullest.

It was the era of the flapper, when liberated girls cut their hair, shortened their skirts, and started smoking and drinking. In England, the rich, young, and elite, labeled the "Bright Young People" by the press, made headlines and filled endless gossip columns with their scandalous costume parties, bathing parties, and midnight scavenger hunts.

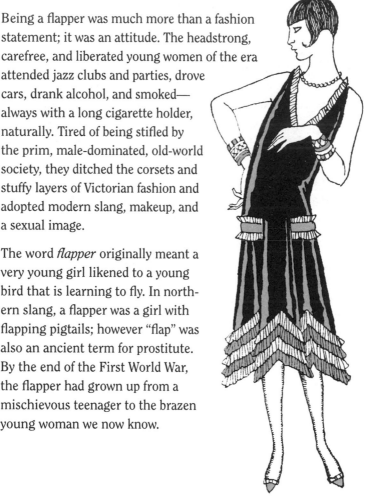

Being a flapper was much more than a fashion statement; it was an attitude. The headstrong, carefree, and liberated young women of the era attended jazz clubs and parties, drove cars, drank alcohol, and smoked—always with a long cigarette holder, naturally. Tired of being stifled by the prim, male-dominated, old-world society, they ditched the corsets and stuffy layers of Victorian fashion and adopted modern slang, makeup, and a sexual image.

The word *flapper* originally meant a very young girl likened to a young bird that is learning to fly. In northern slang, a flapper was a girl with flapping pigtails; however "flap" was also an ancient term for prostitute. By the end of the First World War, the flapper had grown up from a mischievous teenager to the brazen young woman we now know.

...THE FLAPPER AWOKE
FROM HER LETHARGY OF SUB-DEB-ISM,

‹‹‹‹‹‹‹‹‹‹‹‹‹‹‹ ◄◇► ›››››››››››››››

B**OBBED** HER HAIR,

PUT ON HER CHOICEST

PAIR of EARRINGS

‹‹‹‹‹‹‹‹‹‹‹‹‹‹‹ ◄◇► ›››››››››››››››

AND A GREAT DEAL

OF AUDACITY AND ROUGE

and went into the battle.

SHE FLIRTED BECAUSE

IT WAS FUN TO FLIRT.

‹‹‹‹‹‹‹‹‹‹‹‹‹‹‹ ◄◇► ›››››››››››››››

—*from* "EULOGY ON THE FLAPPER" *by Zelda Fitzgerald,*
published in METROPOLITAN *magazine, 1922*

So you want to revive the bold and brazen flapper attitude? Take a cue from these four quintessential flappers who spoke their minds, partied all night, flirted shamelessly, and debunked the strict, old-world ideals of feminism.

ZELDA FITZGERALD Branded as "The First American Flapper" by her husband, F. Scott Fitzgerald, Zelda became the model for the heroines in his bestselling novels, including *The Beautiful and the Damned* and *Tender Is the Night*. Claiming she was no good at anything but "useless pleasure-giving pursuits," Zelda lived for the party lifestyle and drove her husband crazy by stripping off her clothes at parties and flirting with his closest friends.

The couple, who married in 1920 after F. Scott's successful publication of *This Side of Paradise*, were darlings of the New York literary set, socializing with such icons as Dorothy Parker and Ernest Hemingway. Giving birth to their daughter Frances "Scottie" Fitzgerald in 1921 didn't slow them down—they moved to the French Riviera and dazzled and shocked the natives with extravagant parties and outrageous antics.

CLARA BOW Silent film star Clara Bow played her first flapper role in the 1923 movie *Painted People* and went on to play more in such movies as *The Perfect Flapper* (1924) and *Mantrap* (1926). The actress was dubbed "The It Girl" after starring in a movie called *It* (1927), in which she epitomized the wild and seductive flapper. This image carried over to her social life, too, and she became well known in the tabloids for her carefree lifestyle and sexual escapades with fellow movie stars.

Director Frank Lloyd, who cast Bow as high society flapper Janet Oglethorpe in *Black Oxen* (1923), commented: "Bow is the personification of the ideal aristocratic flapper: mischievous, pretty, aggressive, quick-tempered and deeply sentimental."

LOUISE BROOKS Stage and screen actress Louise Brooks's sleek bob and signature fashion sense helped define the flapper look, and her social circle included such influencers as composer George Gershwin and writers F. Scott Fitzgerald, H. L. Mencken, and Anita Loos.

The celebrated actress first appeared in the New York stage productions of *George White's Scandals* and *The Ziegfeld Follies* before launching a film career, which included more than twenty silent movies, with roles that included an immoral femme fatale in *Pandora's Box* (1929) and a disgraced teen in *Diary of a Lost Girl* (1929).

Sadly, the advent of "talkies" led to the end of her career. She then began a new career as a film historian. She died in 1965.

LORELEI LEE The gold-digging heroine of the 1925 novel *Gentlemen Prefer Blondes* was the epitome of the ambitious flapper, as seen through the eyes of author Anita Loos. Loos created the character Lorelei Lee after watching intellectual H. L. Mencken turn to jelly in the presence of a young blonde.

A stunning, amoral dancer who was more concerned with acquiring diamonds and baubles than a wedding ring, Lorelei first appeared in a series of short sketches in *Harper's Bazaar*. The sexual overtones of the "Lorelei Stories" quadrupled the magazine's circulation and led to a bestselling novel. The 1928 movie *Gentlemen Prefer Blondes*, now lost, starred Ruth Taylor as Lorelei, but the 1953 Hollywood remake, starring Marilyn Monroe and Jane Russell, became a classic. The character was later revealed by Loos to be based on Lillian Lorraine, the biggest star of the famous twenties Broadway dance review, *The Ziegfeld Follies*.

Read All About It: *The Flapper* Magazine

For a short run in 1922 flappers had their very own magazine called *The Flapper: Not for Old Fogies*, which hailed from Chicago and championed the new liberated woman. Along with editorials criticizing the "clinging vines" of Victorian sensibilities, *The Flapper* also included articles on health, beauty, and fashion trends. The introductory article in the first issue set the playfully rebellious tone:

> *"Greetings, flappers! All ye who have faith in this world and its people, who do not think we are going to the eternal bowwows, who love life and joy and laughter and pretty clothes and good times, and who are not afraid of reformers, conformers, or chloroformers—greetings! . . . Thanks to the flappers the world is going round instead of crooked, and life is still bearable. Long may the tribe wave!"*

To the WOMAN *» OF THE PERIOD THUS SET FORTH,*

RESTLESS, SEDUCTIVE,
GREEDY, DISCONTENTED,
CRAVING SENSATION,
UNRESTRAINED,
A LITTLE MORBID,
more than a little selfish,

slack of mind as she is trim of body,
NEUROTIC AND VIGOROUS,
a worshipper of tinsel gods at perfumed altars,
fit mate for the hurried, reckless and cynical
man of the age, predestined mother of—what
manner of being?

  I DEDICATE THIS STUDY OF HERSELF.

—Samuel Hopkins Adams's dedication to his novel FLAMING YOUTH
(published under the pseudonym Warner Fabian)

The true flapper shot from the lip, with slang phrases designed to show how hip and modern she was. Here are a few of the popular slang terms of the 1920s, updated for easy use for the modern flapper:

ALARM CLOCK—chaperone
"Maybe we can lose the alarm clock and get out of here . . ."

ALIBI—bunch of flowers
"He came to my door with an alibi of lilies."

APPLEKNOCKER—a yokel or hick
"Who invited the appleknocker?"

APPLESAUCE—flattery
"What do you want? You're full of applesauce."

BANK'S CLOSED—no petting or kisses allowed
"Sorry, sweetheart, bank's closed."

BARNEY-MUGGING—love-making
"If you're lucky, we'll do some barney-mugging later."

BISCUIT—a pettable girl
"He had his eyes on a sweet biscuit across the room."

BLUSHING VIOLET—a publicity hound
"There she goes again, causing a scene like a blushing violet . . ."

CAKE BASKET—limousine
"Look who just rolled up in that fancy cake basket!"

CLOTHES LINE—a neighborhood gossip
"I heard from the clothes line that your goof's back in town."

CORN-SHREDDER—young man who treads on one's feet when dancing

"We spent all night avoiding the corn-shredders on the dance floor."

CRASHER—anyone who comes to a party uninvited

"No crashers allowed."

DAPPER—father

"Sorry! My dapper's our alarm clock tonight!"

DIMBOX—taxi

"Don't worry, we'll catch a dimbox home."

DINGLEDANGLER—a persistent caller on the phone

"If I'd known you were such a dingledangler, I wouldn't have given you my number!"

DOGS—feet

"These shoes make my dogs hurt."

DROPPING THE PILOT—getting divorced

"Did you hear she's finally dropping the pilot?"

DUDDLING UP—getting dressed

"I'll be right down—just duddling up!"

EDISONED—being asked a lot of questions

"Her friends edisoned her about last night's date."

FEATHERS—light conversation

"Exhausted from a raucous weekend, we exchanged feathers at Sunday brunch."

FINALE HOPPER—a man who arrives after the bill is paid

"Everyone knows he's a finale hopper—that's why we don't like to tell him our plans."

FLAT TIRE—dull person

"Don't be such a flat tire—come out with us!"

FORTY-NINER—a man who prospects for a wealthy wife

"He's no forty-niner, I can tell you that. I haven't got a cent to my name!"

GIMLET—a chronic bore

"Oh, please don't invite her. She's such a gimlet, she'll bring us all down."

GOOF—sweetie

"My goof is whisking me away to the beach this weekend."

HEN COOP—beauty parlor

"The girls are all at the hen coop getting bobbed."

HOOCH—liquor

"Pour me some of that hooch!"

HUSH MONEY—allowance from parents

"I think I'll buy a new string of beads with this week's hush money."

LET'S BLOUSE—let's go

"Let's blouse; I'm sick of this static."

MUNITIONS—makeup

"I'm going to the ladies room to freshen my munitions."

MUSTARD PLASTER—an unwelcome man who sticks around

"That mustard plaster followed us from party to party all night, just waiting for an opportunity to approach."

OILCAN—imposter

"She felt like an oilcan when she went shopping with her wealthier friends."

SNUGGLEPUPS—young men at petting parties

"By the time the girls had duddled up and made their way to the party, all the snugglepups were taken."

STATIC—meaningless conversation

"I don't have time for static; just get to the point!"

SUGAR—money

"That man looks like he's got a lot of sugar."

UMBRELLA—a young man any woman can borrow for the evening

"I'll lend you my umbrella for tonight, as long as you don't tire him out for our date tomorrow."

WIND SUCKER—someone who boasts

"They were wind suckers all night after it was announced that they'd won the scavenger hunt."

WURP—killjoy

"Even though everyone else was having fun, she insisted on being a wurp and reminding them of their curfews."

UNIVERSAL TERMS FOR GOOD THINGS:

- ◆ the cat's pajamas
- ◆ the bee's knees
- ◆ the elephant's instep
- ◆ ritzy
- ◆ spiffy
- ◆ swanky
- ◆ swell
- ◆ ducky
- ◆ hotsy-totsy

UNIVERSAL TERMS FOR BAD THINGS:

- ◆ banana oil
- ◆ bunk
- ◆ hokum
- ◆ hooey
- ◆ horse feathers
- ◆ lousy
- ◆ hinky
- ◆ slum
- ◆ pill

Dismissed by many as members of an errant and impetuous counterculture, flappers were frowned upon by society and frequently berated in conservative newspapers and magazines. However, not everyone was so quick to condemn. In his 1924 lecture on psychoanalysis, eminent psychologist Dr. Frank Stanton claimed the flapper was a more honest creature than her mother, and one with more common sense. In an article in the Connecticut paper the *Hartford Daily Courant*, he is reported to have said:

"People have been afraid of admitting their natural longings and have become unhappy and ingrown. The Flapper knows what she wants and goes after it. Her cigarettes and snappy manner are her first feeble symptoms of her declaration of independence. She is fast becoming rationalized as she understands herself better. She is the hope of the future and we should be proud of her."

The cult of the flapper originated in the United States, but by the dawn of the decade, her carefree attitude and party lifestyle had already spread through the drawing rooms of London and infected the wealthy young aesthetes of Chelsea and Mayfair. In postwar Britain, the era of the Bright Young People was born.

Outrageous antics, all-night parties, and high-speed treasure hunts filled the fun-packed days of the Bright Young People. For this small group of artists, writers, and socialites—who came together through mutual friends, family connections, and prized invitations to "frightfully" exclusive parties—London in the 1920s was a playground of hedonism and thrill seeking. Their festivities filled the daily gossip pages in the tabloid press, which gave them their famous nickname, while their elders tutted over their wild behavior and uncaring attitude.

Not all the Bright Young People came from rich aristocratic families and upper-class circles. Many came from the "nouveau riche" set, whose parents had amassed wealth through business or commerce. But despite their inherently snobbish chatter, the Bright Young People gave talented artists and writers the chance to climb up the social ladder and no one benefited more than Cecil Beaton, who would become a celebrated society photographer, and novelist Evelyn Waugh. On marrying into the aristocratic family of his first wife, Evelyn Gardner, the daughter of Lord and Lady Burghclere, Waugh remarked that his mother-in-law was "quite inexpressibly pained" by her daughter's lowly choice.

WHO'S WHO

Leading lights included Elizabeth Ponsonby, Brenda Dean Paul, the Jungman sisters (Zita and Teresa), Bryan Guinness, Brian Howard, brothers Stephen and David Tennant, novelists Anthony Powell, Evelyn Waugh, and Beverley Nichols, artist Cecil Beaton, the Mitford sisters (including Nancy and Diana), and the actress Tallulah Bankhead.

Dashing Young Royals

The Prince of Wales, who would later abdicate from the throne as King Edward VIII, was an unofficial patron of the Bright Young People. The dashing young royal was a frequent guest at the cocktail parties in Mayfair and was often found in London's more exclusive nightclubs. His legendary drinking and womanizing made him the ultimate star of the gossip columns, but his hedonistic lifestyle also made him some enemies in court. In his diaries Alan "Tommy" Lascelles, who worked for the Prince's father, George V, recorded how appalled he was by the heir to the throne's behavior on a trip to Canada in 1927:

> *"Before the end of our Canadian trip that year, I felt in such despair about him that I told Stanley Baldwin (then Prime Minister, and one of our party in Canada) that the Heir Apparent, in his unbridled pursuit of wine and women, and of whatever selfish whim occupied him at the moment, was going rapidly to the devil and would soon become no fit wearer of the British Crown."*

Among the cacophony of parties and jazz clubs, treasure hunts were a favorite activity among the Bright Young People. A *Daily Mail* report in 1924 described couples tearing across the capital in cars, hunting for clues and a final cash prize, calling them a craze that has "captured all smart London."

The treasure hunts led to other amusements, in particular the "scavenger" hunt. Each pair had to obtain certain items before reaching their designated finishing point, and some of the objects required considerable bravado and some excellent connections.

"Scavenger parties became the vogue, which meant we made more of a nuisance of ourselves rather than just being noisy," wrote Barbara Cartland in her memoir. "The first object we collected was the cap of the commissionaire at the Ritz; the next a nameplate from one of the embassies; then we searched a mews for a horse's bridle. We searched and searched but we couldn't find one."

UP TO NO GOOD

The original creators of scavenger hunts found ingenious ways of hiding clues: the legendary Zita and Teresa Jungman once had a clue baked into a loaf of brown bread at the Hovis factory and even persuaded Lord Beaverbrook to print a fake edition of the *Evening Standard* with a clue hidden among made-up news stories.

HOST A
1920s-THEMED SCAVENGER HUNT

Divide friends into teams of two or more and send them on an adventure through your town or city to retrieve five to ten items on the list below, popularized or invented in the 1920s. Set a time for the group to meet back at the party spot, and have a bowl of Roaring '20s Champagne Punch at the ready (recipe follows). Set out celery sticks, bread-sticks, olives, radishes, salted nuts, caviar, and deviled eggs or shrimp cocktail for them to munch on while the points are tallied.

'20s—ERA ITEMS TO PROCURE:

A tube of bright red lipstick—5 POINTS

A Birdseye frozen dinner—5 POINTS

A mah-jongg tile—15 POINTS

An empty bottle of gin—5 POINTS

A video of someone dancing the Charleston on a stage—25 POINTS

Audio of a jazz performance—15 POINTS

A Pez dispenser—5 POINTS

A Band-aid—5 POINTS

A hairnet—5 POINTS

A feather boa—15 POINTS

One slice of prepackaged, presliced bread—5 POINTS

A flask (extra points for a hip flask)—10 TO 25 POINTS

A DVD of a movie released in the '20s
*   (5 extra points for a silent film)*—15 POINTS

An example of art deco style—15 POINTS

A straw or wool fedora (or a photo of someone
*   wearing one)*—15 POINTS

Something with fringe—15 POINTS

ROARING '20s CHAMPAGNE PUNCH

2 cups white sugar	Juice of 2 lemons
1 cup water	2 cups freshly brewed
2 (750 ml) bottles	black tea, chilled
champagne, chilled	2 cups light rum
2 tablespoons orange	4 tablespoons brandy
Curaçao	1 quart soda water

In a small saucepan, bring the sugar and water to a boil over medium heat. Let the mixture boil for about 10 minutes, or until it develops a syrupy consistency. Add the syrup to a punch bowl along with the champagne, Curaçao, lemon juice, tea, rum, and brandy. Mix well and top with the soda water before serving.

IF A FEW PEOPLE

GOT MOBBED UP AND MADE FOOLS OF

IN THE PROCESS [of OUR FUN].

well, it didn't really hurt them.

WE MADE A LOT OF OTHER PEOPLE LAUGH.

QUITE FRANKLY, I THINK THE

<<<<<<<<<<<<<< ◄─◇─► >>>>>>>>>>>>>>

BRIGHT

YOUNG PEOPLE

<<<<<<<<<<<<<< ◄─◇─► >>>>>>>>>>>>>>

BROUGHT *a* GREAT DEAL *of* BRIGHTNESS

TO A WORLD

WHICH WAS STILL SADLY IN NEED OF IT.

—*from* WE DANCED ALL NIGHT *by Barbara Cartland*

The relative innocence of scavenger hunts and childish pranks was soon eclipsed in the gossip pages by the more scandalous antics of some of their more outrageous friends, led by the incorrigible Elizabeth Ponsonby and her openly camp cohorts, most notably Brian Howard. Their antics included illegal drinking at underground nightclubs and outrageous fancy-dress parties, which sent shock waves through polite society.

Looking for trouble? Follow in these bright young footsteps and make your own mischief:

IF YOU'RE GOING TO MISBEHAVE AT PARTIES, WEAR A DISGUISE: At one garden party, which Teresa Jungman attended in the guise of a Russian royal, she met a respected general and his wife, and announced to the general that she would never forget the night she had spent with him in Paris. When he replied, rather crossly, that he had spent only one night in Paris during the war, she quipped, "Zat was ze night."

THE ULTIMATE PRANK: FAKE YOUR OWN WEDDING: Another scandalous prank pulled by the Bright Young People was the mock wedding party held at the Trocadero in 1929. Apparently the brainchild of Elizabeth Ponsonby, who played the part of the not-so-blushing bride, the wedding breakfast featured John Rayner as the groom and Robert Byron as the best man, resplendent in bowler hat and waxed mustache. Oliver Messel was an usher and Babe Plunket Greene a bridesmaid.

One newspaper reported: "It was shortly after one o'clock that the patrons were interested to see the 'bride' arrive, holding a bouquet of perfect pink roses, escorted by a good-looking, but somewhat shy young 'bridegroom,' immaculate from his waved hair to his striped shirt.

"The spirited youngsters then roped in an unsuspecting clergyman, who happened to be enjoying lunch at the Piccadilly restaurant, and asked him to join them. He gave a blessing to the 'newly-weds' who were then showered with confetti and rose petals as they left. The 'bride and bridegroom' left 'for their honeymoon' in an ancient taxi-cab, to which some thoughtful friend had tied an even more ancient shoe."

Their lavish lifestyles and outrageous parties were the talk of London, and earning a place in their exclusive group was a coveted honor. If you're looking to channel the highbrow antics, creative party ideas, and elaborate pranks of the Bright Young People, first get to know these five legendary members of the clique:

The Jungman Sisters—THE ART WORLD INSIDERS

The beautiful Jungman sisters were at the heart of the Bright Young People and enjoyed a celebrated status among the smart set for their inventive escapades. Zita and Teresa, who was known as "Baby" despite her own protests, were the daughters of Dutch artist Nico Jungman and the stepdaughters of Richard Guinness. Mum Beatrice was renowned for her parties, where high society mixed with artists and actresses. At one event in 1926, for instance, tables were laden with caviar, oysters, paté, turkeys, kidneys and bacon, hot lobsters, and meringues, and the guests included Ivor Novello, actresses Gladys Cooper and Tallulah Bankhead, and artist Oliver Messel. See page 76 for details for throwing your own Jungman Red and White Party.

Elizabeth Ponsonby—THE INSTIGATOR

Daughter of politician Arthur Ponsonby, leading London socialite, Elizabeth Ponsonby was one of the founding members of the Bright Young People. Along with her friends Lady Eleanor Smith and Zita and Baby Jungman, she created the first treasure hunt across London. She was also behind the infamous Bath and Bottle Party in 1928 (see page 72).

Art historian John Rothenstein described Elizabeth as a "stylishly slender girl of about twenty-two, with an oval pale face especially modeled, it seemed to me, to express an aristocratic disdain. Already she was something of a legend."

Evelyn Waugh—THE ARCH OBSERVER

The son of a middle-class publisher, Evelyn Waugh was educated at Oxford, where he met many of the future Bright Young People and developed a taste for country house weekends and smart parties. He worked as a schoolmaster before publishing his first novel, *Decline and Fall*, in 1928. Although he was friends with many of the inner circle, Evelyn remained on the outskirts until the late 1920s, acting more as observer than participant. His novels *Brideshead Revisited, Vile Bodies,* and *A Handful of Dust* drew heavily on the characters and experiences of the Bright Young People.

Loelia Ponsonby met the author at Great Cumberland Place, and recalled in *Grace and Favour*, "Evelyn Waugh was a formidable young man who looked like a furious cherub. His glaring eye was watching us. His sharp ear missed nothing. What he said was pungent and he gave one the feeling that he was an unhappy man who found in the world 'much to amuse but little to admire.' "

At school Brian Howard was a founding member of the Eton Society of the Arts, along with Anthony Powell, Harold Acton, and novelist Henry Yorke, and a member of the famed Hypocrites Club at Oxford. A flamboyant homosexual and a sartorial poet, he gained a reputation as one of the most outrageous and influential members of the Bright Young People and was behind many of the practical jokes and outrageous outings of the inner set.

Daphne Weymouth, Marchioness of Bath, described him as "a sinister impresario, with epigrams cracking from his lips and dark eyebrows raised, he looked mockingly down his nose at his protégés dancing like puppets as he pulled the strings."

FURTHER READING: *Start Your Own Roaring Book Club*

Many of the decade's most celebrated writers immortalized flappers and Bright Young People in novels, poetry, and essays, each rendering a unique view of the iconic characters, lavish parties, reckless pranks, societal shifts, and changing times of the Roaring Twenties. Pick a few of the works below and start a 1920s-themed book club. For each meeting, serve Prohibition cocktails (page 84).

The Glimpses of the Moon, by Edith Wharton (1922)

Flappers and Philosophers, by F. Scott Fitzgerald (1921)

Babbitt, by Sinclair Lewis (1922)

The Beautiful and the Damned, by F. Scott Fitzgerald (1922)

The Garden Party and Other Stories, by Katherine Mansfield (1922)

Tales of the Jazz Age, by F. Scott Fitzgerald (1922)

Murder on the Links, by Agatha Christie (1923)

The Plastic Age, by Percy Marks (1924)

The Great Gatsby, by F. Scott Fitzgerald (1925)

The Weary Blues, by Langston Hughes (1926)

The Sun Also Rises, by Ernest Hemingway (1926)

Gentlemen Prefer Blondes, by Anita Loos (1926)

Enough Rope: Poems, by Dorothy Parker (1926)

The Hotel, by Elizabeth Bowen (1927)

Decline and Fall, by Evelyn Waugh (1928)

Vile Bodies, by Evelyn Waugh (1930)

DRESS LIKE
A BRIGHT
YOUNG THING

FASHION

IS NOT SOMETHING THAT EXISTS IN DRESSES ONLY,

FASHION

IS IN THE SKY, IN THE STREET,

FASHION

HAS TO DO WITH IDEAS,

THE WAY WE LIVE

WHAT IS HAPPENING

—*Coco Chanel*

Perhaps the most striking thing about twenties fashion is that it wasn't just about clothes; it was the statement that set the young apart from the old, the rich from the poor, and the "respectable" aristocracy from the Bright Young People. Twenties fashion was a sartorial rebellion and a visible proof that the wearer was a fully signed-up member of what F. Scott Fitzgerald called the "Jazz Age."

This decade also saw the rise of cheaper off-the-rack clothing for both men and women. Men of all classes could now afford to wear stylishly tailored suits of the era, and thanks to department store dresses, affordable women's magazines, and easy-to-make dress patterns, at long last, the ordinary girl could realistically aspire to high style and make it happen—and she did so with gusto and with practical application.

The French designer Coco Chanel was the most influential style icon of the decade. As Joshua Zeitz put it in his book *Flapper*, Chanel was "the right woman, at the right time, in the right place." Her "garçonne" look, created in Paris, soon caught on around the world and inspired the boyish style of the flapper age.

Irritated by the frills and frou-frou of the upper-class female wardrobe, and conscious of the need for practical clothing for women who had worked through the war years and beyond, Chanel set about simplifying haute couture. Using soft jersey, the traditional material for men's underwear, she produced elegant suits, cardigans, and trousers, as well as beaded evening dresses with simple shapes and dropped waistbands. Coco said she came up with the look because she felt it was time to "let go of the waistline." The Chanel suit was heralded as "the new uniform for afternoon and evening."

In 1926, American *Vogue* referred to the Little Black Dress as "Chanel's Ford," meaning it was as popular and as universally available as Henry Ford's mass-produced motorcar.

FLIRTING WITH FASHION:
Wardrobe Flapper Essentials and Accessories

The Shape

To achieve a curve-free, youthful figure, women's formerly prized "hourglass" figures disappeared underneath tubular dresses with dropped waistbands, while the slightly shorter hemline, which reached the mid-calf, allowed for much more freedom of movement. The corset, which had long strained to create the womanly curves of the Victorian and Edwardian eras, was ditched in favor of the looser camisole and brassiere which, in the twenties, offered no support.

The emphasis in fashion design fell to the hips, with sashes or blocks of color highlighting the dropped waistline, and decorative detail, such as fabric flowers, placed to one side. The skirts of the dress were pleated or tiered for daywear and often fringed for the evening, causing a fabulous effect during the all-night dance marathons that were all the rage. The simple sheath dresses were jazzed up with elaborate beading, sequins, and tiny mirrors sewn onto the fabric, creating shimmering visions as the Bright Young Things went about their business.

Many evening dresses were sleeveless, and the more daring socialites risked plunging necklines or backs. The nude effect could also be achieved by the use of sheer materials, such as silk, organza, and chiffon, creating a softer look around the shoulders and arms.

◀ HATS
The cloche hat was a finishing piece for most outfits. The tightly fitted caps rested over the brow, requiring the wearer to tilt her head upward in order to see and made her appear to look snootily down her nose.

BLOUSES ▶
Ladies with larger busts took to bandaging their breasts to flatten and contain them, using tubular, elastic roll-on underwear to keep everything in place.

◀ WAISTLINE
Dropped waistbands take the emphasis off of the traditional (and out-moded) "hourglass" figure.

FABRICS AND PRINTS ▶
Bold geometric shapes and bright colors replaced austere prints from the Victorian era. Comfortable fabrics, such as light jersey and cotton, were favored and allowed women maximum movement.

▼ SHOE CLIPS
It was common practice to attach geometric or brightly studded clips to older shoes. This enabled women to extend their collection and affordably update their look.

STOCKINGS ▶
With the introduction of artificial silk, called rayon, in 1924, flesh-colored stockings entered the fashion scene in beige, cream, and light brown tones that gave a more natural look and showed legs to their best advantage.

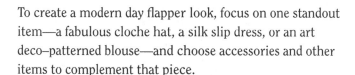

DRESS LIKE A MODERN DAY FLAPPER

To create a modern day flapper look, focus on one standout item—a fabulous cloche hat, a silk slip dress, or an art deco–patterned blouse—and choose accessories and other items to complement that piece.

- Look for a tight-fitting cloche hat or a stylish headband to wear around the crown of your head

- Adorn yourself with feathers, faux fur, or lace to add a hint of extravagance

- Dress in slinky fabrics such as satin or silk or chiffon

- Choose a simple slip dress or one with a drop waist for optimal movement

- Opt for dresses with plunging necklines or backs

- Keep your skirt at or slightly above the knee

- Drape a long scarf over your head or shoulders for a little mystery

- Embrace embellishments: anything fringed, beaded, or jeweled fits perfectly within the flapper theme

- For your feet, keep it comfortable in Mary Jane pumps or Oxford shoes

Must-Have Accessories

JAZZING IT UP The simple, drop-waist dresses could be glammed up for outings with a number of must-have accessories. Art Deco designs were de rigueur and the emphasis shifted to design rather than to the value of decorative items.

FANCY FOOTWORK As dancing was the key to a flapper's lifestyle, high heels were out of the question. Shoes were fairly low, with practical yet modish Cuban or Louis-style (hourglass shape) heels and straps or T-bars across the arch of the foot, similar to those worn by professional Latin and ballroom dancers today.

HEAD CASE The wide-brimmed hats of the previous generation were replaced with silk turbans or close-fitting cloche hats that were pulled low over one's ears. For the evening, a simple band was often worn as a stylish accessory, perhaps with a feather or flower for decoration, or sprinkled with sparkling beads.

DIVINE FINERY A long string of pearls was an essential item in the society flapper's arsenal and looked perfect with the flat-fronted dresses. Fashion-conscious girls on a budget, however, could make do with beads, always worn in long strands. Earrings were also worn long and dangly, and brooches sporting feathers and colorful stones were a popular addition to coats and jackets. At the high end of the market, coral, jade, aquamarine, onyx, and opal replaced the more classic diamonds, and platinum was the latest luxury metal.

Long gloves often accompanied the sleeveless dresses, while long cigarette holders provided an elegant accessory for the girl about town. Feathers were all the rage; the smarter set carried a fan of ostrich feathers to cool down in the evening.

Flappers were pioneers in the makeup department, as they rejected the demure Victorian look for dramatic, smoky eyes, rouged cheeks, and dark red lipstick. Metal lipstick holders had come onto the market in 1915, and they could be easily carried in a handbag. For the first time ever, it became fashionable to touch up makeup in public, with girls fishing out compacts and lip color wherever they sat in the dance halls and tearooms. Follow the beauty tips below to achieve the bold flapper look:

FACE The '20s flapper face began with a foundation of cream or cake, then face powder for a clean matte finish. In the early part of the decade, cream and ivory tones were used for the popular pale look. However, in 1923, after Coco Chanel returned from a beach vacation flaunting a deep suntan, tans—once shunned as the sign of manual labor—became fashionable, and women took to using darker foundations and powders that were closer to their natural skin tones.

CHEEKS Cream or liquid rouge, in rose or berry shades, was applied in circles to the apples of the cheeks. That was followed by a little powder, and then a second layer of powdered rouge to set.

EYES Thick, dark kohl was used around the eyes, with copious mascara employed for the long-lashed look. Eyelids were made to shine with Vaseline and covered with eye shadow in shades of gray, green, black, or turquoise. Eyebrows were thin, black, and directed in downward curves with eyeliner.

LIPS Dark lip liner and deep red lipstick accentuated the vampish flapper look. Twenties film star Clara Bow inspired a craze for cupid's bow lips in the mid-twenties, with her deep red, perfectly sculpted mouth. The look, created by Max Factor from his newly developed Color Harmony line, led to the brand becoming a popular choice with young women, along with Elizabeth Arden.

TO ACHIEVE CUPID'S BOW LIPS:

▶1◀ Cover your lips with concealer or foundation that matches your skin tone.

▶2◀ Using a thick, dark lip liner, trace the curve in your top lip. When your top lip starts to curve downward, veer inside of your natural lip line to create a heart shape.

▶3◀ Fill your lips with red or any dark shade of lipstick, making sure both top and bottom have equal amounts of color.

▶4◀ Finish with lip gloss for a bit of shimmer.

CHOP CHOP!: *Get Your Own Bobbed Look*

For the fashion-forward, this meant cutting her hair short—very short. The liberated woman of the Jazz Age wore her hair in a fashionable bob: either straight and glossy, or "shingled," meaning cut shorter at the nape of the neck in a V-shape. This shorter style caused outrage in the newspapers, spawning headlines such as "Shingle Blow to Marriage" and "Shingles Leave Girls Single."

In the last few years of the decade, variations on the bob gained popularity, namely the slicked back and greased down Eton cut, where curls were "glued" down in front of each ear, and the softer finger wave. Reference the illustrations below for glam flapper inspiration.

Flappers may remain the style icons of the decade, but men of the era also set the stage for modern fashion trends. Before the First World War, young men had adopted cuts of suit similar to those of their older counterparts—but the Jazz Age was all about the celebration of youth, and the Bright Young Things had no intention of dressing like their dads. By the second half of the decade, the formal frock coats and morning suits of a bygone age were replaced with simpler, more relaxed suits that met the needs of the entire day. A well-tailored tuxedo fitted the bill for eveningwear, often worn with modish two-tone lace-up shoes, which became highly fashionable with those chaps who liked to flash their feet while dancing the Charleston.

With the addition of a few wardrobe staples, the modern man can look as dapper as the bright young men of the '20s:

HATS The 1920s gentleman never left the house without a hat. Popular styles included the sophisticated Panama and Boater, the classic Fedora, and the casual or sporty golf cap.

SHIRTS Long-sleeve cotton dress shirts in classic white, stripes, or light colors (such as tan, green, blue, lilac, sage green, yellow, and pink) were the standard for fashionable men of the decade. Toward the end of the decade, attached collars began to be worn in place of the starched detachable ones of the past, and this relic of the Edwardian era slowly had its day.

TIES Bow ties, short, narrow neckties, and ascots were all popular accessories for bright young men. As the decade went on, the colors brightened, featuring art deco designs and bold stripes, polka dots, checks, and plaid.

SUITS Men of the Jazz Age opted for wide, pleated trousers commonly known as "Oxford bags," worn with suspenders and paired with trim single- or double-breasted jackets. Double-breasted vests also rose in popularity, as did brightly colored sweater-vests, for more casual outings.

OXFORD BAGS

In 1925, as a way around the banning of knickers in the university, a group of Oxford undergraduates came up with a new, loose style of flannel trouser. Considered outrageous by the establishment, the Oxford bags—so named for their baggy legs—could measure between 22 and 40 inches at the bottom of the leg and, as a result, could be slipped over the offending knickerbockers with ease.

CASUAL WEAR Men's casual wear in the twenties was influenced by the popularity of hearty outdoor sports, such as golf, tennis, and shooting. As a result, knickerbockers, soon shortened to "knickers," became popular casual wear for the well-dressed gentleman.

Worn with a Norfolk coat—traditionally used for shooting, due to its pleated back for ease of movement—knickers came in four styles: plus fours, plus sixes, plus eights, and plus tens. The number denoted how many inches below the knee the coat hit the trouser leg.

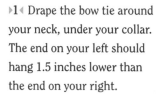

♩PORTING A BOWTIE: *How to Properly Tie One On*

▶1◀ Drape the bow tie around your neck, under your collar. The end on your left should hang 1.5 inches lower than the end on your right.

▶2◀ Cross the longer end over the shorter end.

▶3◀ Pass the longer end up through loop.

▶4◀ Make the front loop of the bow by tugging the shorter, hanging end to the left and then folding it over itself to the right.

▶5◀ While holding the front loop between the thumb and index finger of your left hand, use your right hand to drop the long end down over the front.

▶6◀ Place your right index finger pointing up on the bottom half of the hanging part. Feed the hanging end up behind the front loop.

▶7◀ Tuck the resulting loop through the knot behind the front loop.

▶8◀ Hold the bow at both folded ends and pull carefully to tighten the knot.

(Adapted from www.brooksbrothers.com/tieknots/bowtie.tem)

HOOK UP

(and get hitched)

I FEEL QUITE SURE,

AN AFFAIRE

D'AMOUR

Would be >>>
ATTRACTIVE
While we're
STILL
ACTIVE,
≡ LET'S ≡
MISBEHAVE!

—*Cole Porter,* "LET'S MISBEHAVE"

A ROARING
VIEW OF MARRIAGE

Despite a seemingly frivolous attitude to marriage, the Bright Young People did expect to walk down the aisle for real at some point. In a world where the majority of careers were still closed to women, a good marriage was the most they could look forward to and magazines of the day were desperate to convince the young, independent woman that marriage was "the best job of all."

THE NOT-SO-VIRGIN BRIDE

A survey by American biologist Alfred Kinsey found that 50 percent of women born between 1900 and 1909 were not virgins on their wedding day, compared to around 25 percent before the First World War. The majority of those women, however, had had sex only with their fiancés.

As more single women went out to work, the journals of the day began reluctantly to accept the situation, but saw paid employment as a pathway to marriage. *Woman's Own*, for example, suggested that becoming a nurse, a library assistant, or a secretary could provide "a short cut to a prosperous marriage." The best occupation, in their opinion, was telephonist, because "many a man falls in love with a voice."

For her walk down the aisle, the flapper bride chose a simple, tea-length, loose-cut chemise or tube dress, with Mary Jane or T-strap heels, a single string of pearls, and an elaborate headpiece or veil to feminize her close-cropped haircut.

WEDDING GOWNS In 1920, Coco Chanel introduced a short, knee-length dress with a long train, which also cemented white, a popular choice already, as the universal color of the wedding dress.

CAP VEILS Made from luxurious silk tulle or lace and fitted around the crown of the head, cap veils were all the rage. Other popular headpieces were wreathes made of either natural materials or gilded fabrics, and tight-fitting cloche hats.

WEDDING RINGS Matched engagement and wedding bands were the height of fashion in the '20s, and square or lace mounts replaced the diamond solitaires of previous years. Plain gold bands were ditched in favor of carved designs, which were considered more youthful—a must if the Bright Young Things were to wed at all.

Get to know the provocative duos who sensationalized the conventions of marriage.

Zelda AND F. Scott Fitzgerald

F. Scott Fitzgerald and his wife Zelda hosted epic parties and lived lavishly off of Fitzgerald's writing career, becoming the golden couple of the Jazz Age. But they were more than just partiers; they also became members of the intellectual set, rubbing elbows with fellow influencers Ernest Hemingway, Dorothy Parker, and Gertrude Stein. A year after the couple was married, Fitzgerald wrote his second novel, *The Beautiful and the Damned*. Three years later, after their daughter Scottie was born, he completed his best-known work, *The Great Gatsby*.

Before long, though, the couple's extravagant, smart-set lifestyle caught up with them, and Fitzgerald's alcoholism and Zelda's mental illness (the subject of Fitzgerald's fourth novel, *Tender tIs the Night*) took a toll on the marriage. Zelda was in and out of clinics from 1930 until her death in 1948, during which time F. Scott moved to Hollywood to pursue a screenwriting career. He died in 1940.

Mary Pickford AND Douglas Fairbanks

In 1920 the sweetheart of the silver screen, Mary Pickford, married Douglas Fairbanks, the dashing star of such swashbuckling adventures as *The Mask of Zorro*. Their honeymoon in London and Paris caused riots, as fans jostled to see Hollywood's most glamorous couple, and their return to the United States brought huge crowds to railway stations across the country to catch a glimpse of their idols, who were now "Hollywood royalty."

An invitation to Pickfair, their Beverly Hills mansion, was the most sought-after ticket in town, and dignitaries from the White House often asked if it was possible to visit. Dinner guests at Pickfair included George Bernard Shaw, Noël Coward, H. G. Wells, F. Scott Fitzgerald, Sir Arthur Conan Doyle, Albert Einstein, Lord Mountbatten, and aviator Amelia Earhart. Charlie Chaplin, Fairbanks's best friend, was a frequent guest.

The couple's careers suffered with the advent of talking movies, and they split in the early thirties after Fairbanks's affair with English socialite Lady Sylvia Ashley.

Prince Albert AND Lady Elizabeth

The marriage of Prince Albert, Duke of York, to Lady Elizabeth Bowes-Lyon—later to become King George VI and Queen Elizabeth—was the British society wedding of the 1920s. The bride was technically a commoner, so the blessing of the Royal Family and the political establishment signaled a more liberal outlook toward the old conventions.

The couple married on April 26, 1923, in Westminster Abbey, breaking with tradition by choosing a London church rather than a Royal chapel in the well-founded belief that postwar society would have its spirits lifted by a public spectacle. The bride made a touching gesture in remembrance of the war dead, surprising guests by laying her bouquet at the Tomb of the Unknown Soldier. The wedding was also the first to be filmed, although the BBC was not allowed to broadcast it, as the couple had hoped.

Agatha AND Colonel Archie Christie

When writer Agatha Christie was told by Colonel Archie Christie, her husband of twelve years, that he was having an affair and no longer loved her, she took the perfect revenge. In December 1926, she left her home, abandoned her car at Guildford, and "disappeared." In fact she was staying at a hotel in Harrogate under the false name of Miss Neale—the name of her husband's lover.

The eleven days in which the well-known novelist was missing put the spotlight firmly on her errant husband and even led to speculation he had murdered her. The newspapers had a field day and Archie suffered huge social embarrassment. They eventually divorced in 1928.

Single flappers may have been shocking society with their disreputable behavior, but in truth the majority of them were quite chaste compared to some of their married counterparts. The Bright Young People's public displays of uproarious rebellion filled the gossip columns—but the real scandals of the 1920s were taking place behind closed doors . . .

He-Evelyn and She-Evelyn

In June 1928, Evelyn Waugh wed Evelyn Gardner at St. Paul's Church in Portman Square, London, despite vocal opposition from the bride's mother, Lady Burghclere. Among those present were Harold Acton, Robert Byron, Waugh's brother Alec, and Miss Gardner's friend Pansy Pakenham, but the ill-fated marriage lasted no more than a year.

She-Evelyn was taken ill on a Mediterranean cruise the following summer and shortly afterward returned to London, while He-Evelyn repaired to the country to write *Vile Bodies*. A month later, she informed her husband she had fallen in love with Jonathan Heygate, an aristocratic BBC announcer, and she promptly moved her belongings into her lover's flat. Heygate was consequently forced out of the BBC for his part in the divorce. "I did not know it was possible to be so miserable and live," a devastated Waugh said to Harold Acton about his wife leaving him.

The Bolter

Idina Sackville traveled to Kenya with second husband Captain Charles Gordon after their marriage in 1919, and quickly took to the hedonistic lifestyle, taking a stream of lovers from the Muthaiga Country Club.

When her marriage foundered, she returned to her home in London, where she caused further scandal by embarking on a high-profile affair with Josslyn Hay, Earl of Erroll, whom she married in 1923. Together they traveled back to Kenya, where it transpired that Hay, eight years her junior, was as promiscuous as his new wife.

The pair hosted all-night parties at their sprawling bungalow above the Rift Valley, and Idina was said to welcome her guests in a bathtub made of green onyx, before dressing in front of them.

After numerous affairs they split in 1930. Idina, thought to be the model for the character named "The Bolter" in three of Nancy Mitford's novels, would go on to marry twice more.

While drugs were not widespread among the Bright Young Things, homosexuality—at that time still illegal and considered the worst kind of debauchery by the popular press—was rife. Many, like Brian Howard, Stephen Tennant, Beverley Nichols, and Eddie Gathorne-Hardy, were flamboyant peacocks who made no secret of their preferences among their closest friends. Nichols, for example, openly boasted to Cecil Beaton of his flings with writers Somerset Maugham, Oliver Messel, and Noël Coward. Others, like Cole Porter, were married to provide an outward air of respectability while continuing homosexual activity—with or without spousal consent.

At universities and private schools, the sexually confused often went through a "gay phase," seeing experimenting as a rite of passage. Evelyn Waugh, for example, had various affairs with men at Oxford before falling for a succession of high society women. As John Betjeman once remarked, as quoted in Paula Byrne's biography of Waugh, *Mad World*: "Everyone in Oxford was homosexual at that time."

Jazz Gigolos

American songwriter Cole Porter maintained a lavish apartment in Paris, with walls covered in zebra hide, where he and his wife, Linda Lee Thomas, threw their decadent parties. Despite being an outwardly devoted husband, Porter was gay, and according to one biographer, J. X. Bell, his parties were notorious for "gay and bisexual activity, Italian nobility, cross-dressing, international musicians, and a large surplus of recreational drugs."

Throughout the twenties and into the thirties, Leslie "Hutch" Hutchinson was the talk of society drawing rooms throughout London and Paris. The pianist's affairs with rich men and women caused numerous scandals, and Cole Porter, reputed to be one of his many lovers, is thought to have based the 1929 song "I'm a Gigolo" on Hutch.

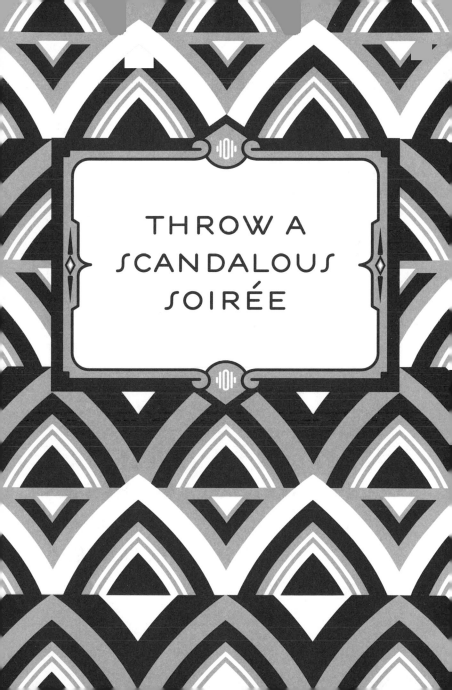

THROW A SCANDALOUS SOIRÉE

MASKED

PARTIES,

SAVAGE PARTIES,

VICTORIAN PARTIES,

≪≪≪≪≪≪≪≪≪≪ ◄◆► ≫≫≫≫≫≫≫≫≫≫

GREEK

≪≪≪≪≪≪≪≪≪≪ ◄◆► ≫≫≫≫≫≫≫≫≫≫

WILD WEST PARTIES,

RUSSIAN PARTIES, CIRCUS PARTIES, *parties where one had to dress as somebody else, almost naked parties in St. John's Wood,* ◄◆►

PARTIES

IN FLATS AND STUDIOS

AND HOUSES AND SHIPS

AND HOTELS AND NIGHT CLUBS

IN WINDMILLS AND SWIMMING-BATHS,

tea parties at school where one ate muffins and meringues and tinned crab, parties at Oxford where one drank brown sherry and smoked Turkish cigarettes,

PARTIES,

DULL DANCES IN LONDON

AND COMIC DANCES IN SCOTLAND

AND DISGUSTING

DANCES IN PARIS

—from VILE BODIES *by Evelyn Waugh*

The 1920s were a time to throw caution and consideration to the wind and party. As long as it was wild, decadent, completely over the top, and exuberant, it was in. Perhaps more than in any other decade, the youth in the twenties expressed an explosion of joie de vivre after WWI, shocking their stiff-upper-lip parents who held prim Victorian morality as the ideal. Themed celebrations became the order of the day, as the Bright Young Things discovered the age of revelry.

Evelyn Waugh's second novel, *Vile Bodies,* is a satire on the lifestyle of the Bright Young People. In the book, Waugh's hero, Adam Fenwick-Symes, lists an array of lavish themed celebrations, many of which were actual events attended by the Mayfair set. The gatherings became increasingly scandalous as each host vied to outdo the last.

BATH AND BOTTLE PARTY

The four brightest lights of the Bright Young People were joint hosts of arguably the most outrageous evening of them all—the Bath and Bottle Party. Babe Plunket Greene, Elizabeth Ponsonby, Eddie Gathorne-Hardy, and Brian Howard hired St. George's swimming baths on Buckingham Palace Road, asking guests to "please wear a Bathing Suit and bring a bath towel and a Bottle." The party, which took place in the sweltering summer of 1928, caused uproar among the chattering classes.

EXTRA, EXTRA

The *Sunday Chronicle* reported of the infamous event: "Great astonishment and not a little indignation is being expressed in London over the revelation that in the early hours of yesterday morning a large number of society women were dancing in bathing dresses to the music of a band at a 'swim and dance' gathering organized by some of Mayfair's Bright Young People." Tom Driberg, in the *Daily Express*' "Talk of London" column, gave an eyewitness account of the event, revealing that some revelers had two or three costumes that they changed into over the course of the evening, which began at eleven p.m. and went on until the early hours. "Cocktails were served in the gallery," he wrote, "where the cocktail-mixers evidently found the heat intolerable, for they also donned bathing costumes at the earliest opportunity."

When the police came to break things up the following morning, where the scantily clad guests were astonishing ordinary people on their way to work, some of the more spirited revelers attempted to drag the unfortunate officers into the changing room in the hope of disrobing them.

THROW YOUR OWN
BATH AND BOTTLE PARTY

All you really need for an unforgettable event is a signature cocktail. Created for the original Bath and Bottle Party, the Bathwater Cocktail is the perfect libation for any summer party.

MAKE YOUR OWN
BATHWATER DRINKIE-POO

1 ounce Amaretto

1 ounce Southern Comfort

1 ounce blue Curaçao

2 ounces cranberry juice

2 ounces pineapple juice

Shake all ingredients vigorously together with ice, strain into a chilled glass, and garnish.

To celebrate the original theme even further, invite your guests for a midnight swim (if you or a friend owns a pool) and instruct them to bring a bottle of champagne. You could also throw this party near a lake, or when vacationing by the beach.

RED AND WHITE PARTY

The Red and White Party, thrown in the house of dancer Maud Allan by the art dealer Arthur Jeffress in conjunction with the notorious Bankhead sisters, began at eleven p.m. on November 21, 1929, and was, according to John Montgomery's 1957 book, *The Twenties,* "the last hectic party of the twenties, the party to end all parties, surpassing even the Wild West party and the Court party." The invitations, white on a bright scarlet background, were so sought after that many were stolen from mantelpieces and used by gatecrashers on the night. Guests at the "monster ball" were instructed to wear only red and white, and the host greeted them in a white sailor suit with red trimmings, white gloves loaded with diamonds, and a muff made of white narcissi.

"Three large rooms in the spacious house had been decorated, with the central space draped in swathes of scarlet and white cloth, a white room for a bar and a red room, complete with mattresses, for 'sitting out.'" The riotous party, which went on until dawn, ended with a few people stripping off and one girl—apparently Brenda Dean Paul—being prevented from pulling the hair of another young beauty as they clashed at the drinks table. Montgomery observed: "The girl was wearing only a choker of pearls and a large red and white spotted handkerchief fixed around her middle by a thin white belt. People wearing more clothes found it almost unbearably hot."

RED AND WHITE PARTY

MENU

APPETIZER:

Red Caviar

FISH COURSE:

Lobster and Salmon

MEAT COURSE:

Roast Ham with Apples

VEGETABLE:

Tomato Salad

DESSERT:

Blanc Mange *(recipe follows)*, trifles, and jellies

DRINKS:

Champagne, white or red wine, and gin
(absolutely no brown liquors)

ALMOND BLANC MANGE WITH RASPBERRY PRESERVES

Makes ¾ cup

½ cup almond milk

1⅛ teaspoons orange flower water

¾ teaspoon almond extract

2 tablespoons simple syrup *(see page 86 for recipe)*

1 tablespoon plus 1 teaspoon heavy cream

1 teaspoon powdered gelatin

Raspberry preserves, for serving

▶1◀ In a 2-cup measuring cup, stir together almond milk, orange flower water, almond extract, simple syrup, and heavy cream. *(You should have ¾ cup total liquid.)*

▶2◀ In a small bowl, sprinkle gelatin over 1 tablespoon water and let stand until softened, at least 5 minutes. In a microwave oven on high power, heat softened gelatin until just melted, 5 to 10 seconds.

▶3◀ Stir gelatin into almond milk mixture until combined. Let sit, gently stirring occasionally, until mixture thickens to the consistency of heavy cream.

▶4◀ Serve with a tablespoon of raspberry preserves.

(Adapted from Fanny Farmer's *The Boston Cooking-School Cook Book*)

PARTY LIKE A BRIGHT YOUNG THING:
THEMES *for Your* NEXT FÊTE

More fabulous themed party ideas from the 1920s:

COME AS YOU WERE TWENTY YEARS AGO:
Guests must dress as their twenty-years-younger selves
(even if it means coming in diapers). David Tennant was
the first to host one of these gatherings, and one of his
guests arrived in a dress from 1906 and was pushing a
stroller that contained her grown daughter in baby clothes.
The band dressed in Eton suits and caps.

THE GREAT URBAN DIONYSIA: Ask guests to visit
their local art museum or peruse www.metmuseum.org
for costume inspiration and accessories for this Greek
costume party. This party was originally thrown in honor
of Brian Howard for his twenty-fourth birthday.

IMPERSONATION PARTY: Guests should come
dressed as well-known personalities, or, for more fun, as
another invited guest. Captain Neil McLachlan originally
threw this party in his Brooke Street home, with a few of
the trendier guests choosing to come as each other (some
even dyeing their hair to complete the costume).

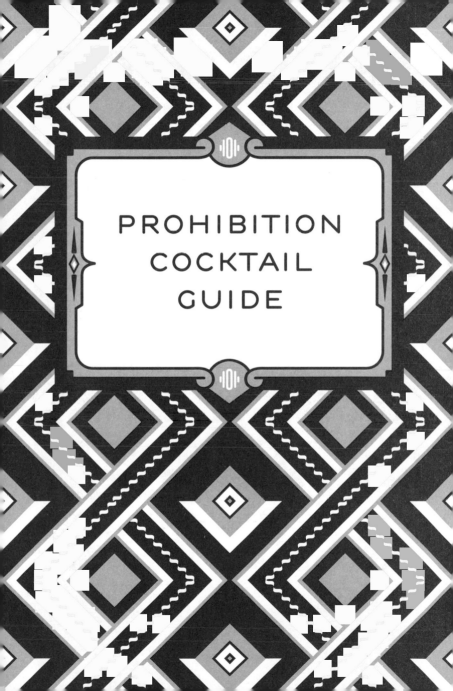

PROHIBITION COCKTAIL GUIDE

THE HOTEL DU CAP

AT ANTIBES

was almost deserted.

<<<<<<<<<<<<<<< ◄◆► >>>>>>>>>>>>>>>

THE HEAT OF DAY LINGERED

IN THE BLUE AND WHITE BLOCKS

of the balcony and from the great canvas mats

OUR FRIENDS

had spread along the terrace

WE WARMED ‹‹‹OUR››› *sunburned backs*

AND

INVENTED NEW COCKTAILS.

—*F. Scott and Zelda Fitzgerald, from* SHOW MR. AND MRS. F.
TO NUMBER——, *a joint account of their travels in Europe*

THE
FIRST MIXOLOGISTS

The popularity of cocktails soared in the twenties, when the manufacture and sale of alcohol was banned in the States and illegally distilled spirits had to be drowned in fruit juices, cream, and soda to make them vaguely palatable. While Prohibition, begun in 1919, succeeded in reducing the overall consumption of liquor, it also gave booze a new glamour. The brightly colored cocktails, with their olive garnish and fancy straws, became the illicit pleasure of those "in the know," and underground clubs, or speakeasies, sprang up all over the United States, allowing organized crime to flourish on the vast profits.

As the sweet whiff of cocktails wafted over the Atlantic, the Mayfair set adopted the new tipples with their usual gay abandon. Cocktail parties became the norm in the early twenties, to the arch disapproval of many of the more conservative middle classes, who felt the influence of the Americans was going too far.

CRIMINAL BEHAVIOR: *Bathtub Gin and Bootleg Booze*

Whiskey and gin brewed in outhouses and backrooms kept the speakeasies going. The clear spirits distilled from cheap grain alcohol, with added water and juniper berries, or glycerin, became known as "bathtub gin." Despite popular belief, the alcohol wasn't fermented in a bathtub at all. The term referred to the fact that the bottles used were too tall to be filled from a tap in the sink, so they had to be topped off with water from the tap in the tub.

At the same time a lucrative trade in "rum-running" sprang up, with smugglers bringing in cheap rum from the Caribbean. Many soon realized that higher profits could be made by smuggling Canadian whiskey, British gin, and French champagne, keeping the likes of the fizz-loving Fitzgeralds expensively sozzled.

THE REAL MCCOY

Pirate Captain Bill McCoy made a fortune from smuggling Caribbean rum into the States via the Atlantic Ocean. The bottles he delivered, being of the highest quality brands, became known as "the real McCoy."

Underground drinking brought many risks, and not just of being busted. Some of the concoctions were more likely to put you in a hospital bed than in a police cell. Here are a few of the most toxic tipples of the era:

- YACK YACK BOURBON—**burnt sugar and iodine made in Chicago, where Al Capone ruled the roost. Burned the throat rather than quenching a thirst.**

- PANTHER WHISKEY—**with a high concentration of fuel oil this could put a tiger in your tank. In fact, it was thought to trigger hallucinations, sexual depravity, paranoia, and murderous impulses.**

- APPLEJACK **an apple brandy distilled from fermented cider by allowing it to freeze and then removing ice chunks. This method resulted in dangerously high levels of methanol and ethanol.**

- SODA POP MOON—**a strong Moonshine created in Philadelphia from rubbing alcohol, commonly used as an antiseptic.**

- JACKASS WHISKEY—**distilled from fruit, sugar, and wheat, it was known to cause internal bleeding.**

- JAKE—**a fluid extract of Jamaican ginger, at over 70 percent proof, the liquor caused paralysis and often death. The dragging gait of a partially paralyzed user became known as the "Jake Walk" or "Jake Leg."**

While cocktails were frowned upon by many, their fruity and creamy content masked the harsh homemade liquors of the time, making them a huge hit with the speakeasy crowd. Here are a few classics for your next Jazz Age soirée:

GIN RICKEY

Fitzgerald's preferred tipple was gin and his favorite cocktail was a "Gin Rickey," made with lime juice.

2 ounces gin
¾ ounce fresh lime juice
Club soda
Slice of lime

Pour the gin and lime juice into a chilled highball glass filled with ice cubes. Top with club soda, and stir gently. Garnish with the slice of lime.

THE ORANGE BLOSSOM

The sugar in this favorite flapper drinkie-poo masked the bitter taste of the bathtub gin.

- **2 ounces gin**
- **1 ounce orange juice**
- **1 teaspoon sugar**
- **1 slice orange**

Mix the gin, orange juice, and sugar in a shaker filled halfway with ice cubes. Shake well, and strain into a cocktail glass. Garnish with the slice of orange.

PINK LADY

A potentially lethal mixture of bathtub gin, apple juice, and egg white, this was a speakeasy favorite.

- **1½ ounces gin**
- **1½ ounces apple juice**
- **Juice of half a lemon**
- **1 fresh egg white**
- **2 dashes grenadine**
- **1 apple slice, for garnish**

Shake all ingredients vigorously together with ice, strain into a chilled glass, and garnish with the apple slice.

WHITE LADY

This frothy drink was invented by Harry MacElhone, an American bartender who fled from New York to London, and later to Paris, to escape Prohibition. He became a key player in the cocktail craze abroad.

2 ounces London dry gin
½ ounce Cointreau
½ ounce fresh lemon juice
1 fresh egg white

Combine all ingredients in a cocktail shaker with some cracked ice, and shake well. Strain into a chilled cocktail glass.

MINT JULEP

Though it originated in the early 1800s, this drink found new fame in 1925, with a mention in F. Scott Fitzgerald's THE GREAT GATSBY.

½ ounce simple syrup
(see below)
2 sprigs fresh mint
2 ounces bourbon

To make the simple syrup, combine ½ cup of sugar and ½ cup of water in a medium saucepan. Bring to a boil and remove when sugar dissolves. Allow to cool before using.

Muddle one sprig of mint in the bottom of a mixing glass with the simple syrup. Add the bourbon, and strain into a highball glass filled with crushed ice. Stir well. Garnish with the remaining sprig of mint.

THE BEE'S KNEES

A spoonful of honey took the edge off the bathtub gin in this sweet-tart concoction.

1½ ounces gin
¾ ounce honey syrup
1 teaspoon fresh lemon
   juice

To make the honey syrup, mix equal parts honey with boiling water; stir until dissolved. In a cocktail shaker filled halfway with ice, combine the syrup, gin, and lemon juice. Shake well. Strain into a cocktail glass.

FRENCH 75

The original recipe for this Prohibition favorite was published in THE SAVOY COCKTAIL BOOK *in 1930. Though the classic version calls for gin, later recipes went with cognac instead.*

2 ounces dry gin
½ ounce lemon juice
¼ ounce simple syrup
   (see page 86 for recipe)
5 ounces champagne
Orange zest

Combine gin, lemon juice, and sugar syrup in a cocktail shaker with ice, and shake well. Strain into a champagne glass. Top it off with the champagne, and garnish with orange zest.

SIDECAR

This classic cocktail is thought to have been invented toward the end of World War I. The first recipes for the Sidecar appear in 1922, in Harry MacElhone's HARRY'S ABC OF MIXING COCKTAILS *and Robert Vermeire's* COCKTAILS: HOW TO MIX THEM.

¾ ounce fresh lemon juice, plus more for the glass
2 tablespoons white sugar
¾ ounce Cointreau
1½ ounces cognac

Rub the outside rim of a cocktail glass with lemon juice and dip it into the sugar. Add the ¾ ounce of lemon juice, the Cointreau, and the cognac to a cocktail shaker filled halfway with cracked ice, and shake well. Strain into the prepared glass.

THE LAST WORD

This concoction was first developed in the early 1920s at the Detroit Athletic Club.

¾ ounce gin
¾ ounce fresh lime juice
¾ ounce green Chartreuse
¾ ounce maraschino liqueur

Pour all of the ingredients into a cocktail shaker filled halfway with ice. Shake well. Strain into a chilled cocktail glass.

BRONX COCKTAIL

Essentially a perfect martini with a splash of orange juice, the Bronx Cocktail was first printed in William "Cocktail" Boothby's 1908 book THE WORLD'S DRINKS AND HOW TO MIX THEM.

- **2 ounces gin**
- **½ teaspoon sweet red vermouth**
- **½ teaspoon dry vermouth**
- **1 ounce orange juice**

Fill a cocktail shaker halfway with ice. Add the gin, both vermouths, and orange juice. Shake well, and strain into a chilled cocktail glass.

THE MARY PICKFORD

Created by '20s mixologist Eddie Woelke—who, like many other bartenders, fled to Havana during Prohibition—the Mary Pickford is pretty and sweet, just like the movie starlet who inspired it.

- **1½ ounces light rum**
- **1 ounce unsweetened pineapple juice**
- **¼ ounce maraschino liqueur**
- **¼ ounce grenadine**
- **Maraschino cherry, for garnish**

Fill a cocktail shaker halfway with ice. Add the rum, pineapple juice, maraschino liqueur, and grenadine. Shake vigorously for at least 30 seconds; then strain into a martini glass. Garnish with the cherry.

DANCE
ALL NIGHT

THE JAZZ AGE

J azz transformed nightlife across the Western world, especially in London, Paris, and American cities such as New York, Chicago, and of course, New Orleans. But the Jazz Age was not just about the music—it was the soundtrack to a way of life that included late-night drinking clubs, cocktails, lush living, gambling, and most of all, dancing.

BY AND LARGE, JAZZ HAS ALWAYS BEEN LIKE THE KIND OF A MAN YOU WOULDN'T WANT YOUR DAUGHTER TO ASSOCIATE WITH.

—Duke Ellington, quoted in AT THE JAZZ BAND BALL: SIXTY YEARS ON THE JAZZ SCENE *by Nat Hentoff*

Through the creativity of musicians such as Jelly Roll Morton, Louis Armstrong, and Duke Ellington (who was considered the most influential player in bringing jazz to the mainstream), the jazz movement quickly spread from New Orleans to New York, and there became part of the Harlem Renaissance, an explosion of African American literature, art, and music, which soon caught the attention of white writers and composers—and ultimately led to the runaway popularity of jazz among the trendsetters of the day.

Until 1922, record companies shied away from putting African American artists on vinyl. Vaudeville star Mamie Smith became the first African American to make a commercial record, when she recorded "Crazy Blues" and "It's Right Here for You" with Okeh Records in 1920.

The success of these recordings led to many more companies, such as Columbia and Paramount, seeking out black jazz artists. Classic releases of the decade include recordings by Jelly Roll Morton and his Red Hot Peppers from 1926 to 1928, and Louis Armstrong's Hot Five and Hot Seven from 1925 to 1928.

SINGING THE BLUES

Bessie Smith, known as the Empress of the Blues, made her first recording in 1923. "Downhearted Blues" sold 780,000 copies in the first six months after its release. Frank Walker was working for Columbia Records when she came into the studio.

"She looked anything but a singer . . . tall and fat and scared to death," he said in Lucy Moore's *Anything Goes*, but added that when she began to sing, "I had never heard anything like the torture and torment she put into the music of her people. It was the blues, and she meant it."

ROARING '20ſ PLAYLIſTſ

Whether you play them to jazz up a speakeasy bash, to learn the Charleston (page 97), or to recover from a raucous weekend, these songs will transport you to the era that forever changed the music scene.

TUNES FOR A BIG NIGHT OUT

"I Wanna Be Loved by You" —Helen Kane

"Button Up Your Overcoat!" —Ruth Etting

"The Varsity Drag" —George Olsen

"Ain't We Got Fun" —Van and Schenck

"Get Low-Down Blues" —Benny Moten's Kansas City Orchestra

"East St. Louis Toodle-Oo" —Duke Ellington

"Charleston" —Arthur Gibbs

"I'm Nobody's Baby" —Marion Harris

"Minnie the Moocher" —Cab Calloway

"Moanin' Low" —The Charleston Chasers

"Jackson Stomp" —Mississippi Mud Steppers

"Nobody Knows You When You're Down and Out" —Bessie Smith

"Diga Diga Doo" —The Mills Brothers

"I'm Looking over a Four Leaf Clover" —Nick Lucas

"Aux Iles Hawaii" —Josephine Baker

"Some of These Days" —Bing Crosby

"I've Got the World on a String" —Louis Armstrong

"The Moon Shines on the Moonshine" —Bert Williams

"Runnin' Wild" —Duke Ellington

"Keep a Song in Your Soul" —Mamie Smith

"Variety Stomp" —Fletcher Henderson

"Black Beauty" —Duke Ellington

"Black Bottom Stomp" —Jelly Roll Morton

"Don't Forget to Mess Around" —Louis Armstrong

"Dinah" —Josephine Baker

"Bye-Bye Blackbird" —Gene Austin

"Let's Do It (Let's Fall in Love)" —Dorsey Brothers Orchestra

"'Deed I Do" —Ben Pollack

"Keep Sweeping the Cobwebs off the Moon" —Ruth Etting

"Hello Montreal" —The Jazz Pilots

"Black and Tan Fantasy" —Duke Ellington

"Crazy Blues" —Mamie Smith

"Corrine Corrina" —Bo Carter

"There Ain't No Maybe in My Baby's Eyes" —Franklyn Baur

"Fussy Mabel" —Jelly Roll Morton

"Exactly like You" —Louis Armstrong

"I'm Crazy 'Bout My Baby" —Fats Waller

"Ain't She Sweet" —Gene Austin

"Let's Misbehave" — Irving Aaronson

"Makin' Whoopee" —Eddie Cantor

"Ain't Misbehavin'" —Fats Waller

"Heebie Jeebies" —Louis Armstrong

"Stormy Weather (Keeps Rainin' All the Time)" —Ethel Waters

"Downhearted Blues" —Bessie Smith

"I'm Gonna Lose Myself Way Down in Louisville" —Alberta Hunter

"Lazy" —Al Jolson

"Am I Blue" —Libby Holman

"My Blue Heaven" — Gene Austin

"Empty Bed Blues" —Bessie Smith

"Rhapsody in Blue" —George Gershwin

"Blue Skies" —Harry Richman

"It Had to Be You" —Isham Jones

"Stardust" —Hoagy Carmichael

"Someone to Watch over Me" —Gertrude Lawrence

"Me and My Shadow" —Helen Morgan

"Breezing Along with the Breeze" —The Revelers

A CHORUS OF DISAPPROVAL

Women's magazines published frequent articles about the evils of jazz, and in December 1921 the *Ladies' Home Journal* printed a piece by John R. McMahon in which dance professional Fenton T. Bott claimed that "jazz is worse than the saloon." He continued: "Those moaning saxophones and the rest of the instruments with their broken, jerky rhythm make a purely sensual appeal. We have seen the effect of jazz music on our young pupils. It makes them act in a restless and rowdy manner."

In the frenzy of fun that followed the war, the traditional waltz and the foxtrot—classic ballroom dances usually performed "in hold"—were replaced with the less stuffy moves of the Shimmy, the Black Bottom, and the dance that epitomized the era most of all: the Charleston.

The original dance was developed by African Americans in the United States in the early part of the twentieth century, and was first seen on the Broadway stage in 1922 and 1923, when the steps appeared in *The Ziegfeld Follies* and the Irving C. Miller production *Liza*.

American dancer Bee Jackson took it on tour with various engagements in New York, California, Paris, and London. Billed as "the champion shimmy shaker and Charleston dancer from America," the young hoofer was a huge hit in the cabaret at London's Piccadilly Hotel and a favorite at the nearby Kit Cat Club.

▶1◀ Find a jazzy tune with a 4/4 beat, such as "Ain't She Sweet," "I Wanna Be Loved by You," or, of course, "Charleston."

▶2◀ Step back with your right foot; then kick back with your left foot.

▶3◀ Step forward with your left foot; (you should be back where you started); then kick forward with your right foot.

▶4◀ Repeat as quickly as you can to the tempo of the music.

▶5◀ When you've got the steps down, add arm motions. Swing your left arm forward and your right arm back when you begin the kick step. It's the same arm motion as when you're walking — just exaggerate the motion, and swing those arms high.

PROHIBITION

has set many dull feet dancing...

THE DISAPPEARANCE OF THE "SPEAKEASY" WOULD
BE AN INFINITE LOSS TO ALL ROMANTICISTS.

WHO, *having slunk down the little flight of stairs into the area, glancing to right and left, in order to make sure no police are watching, having blinked at the sudden lighted grille and assured the proprietor, whose face peers through the bars, of his bona fides—who would willingly forfeit these delicious preliminaries?*

AND WHO, *having taken his seat in the shuttered restaurant, having felt all the thrill of the conspirator, having jumped at each fresh ring of the bell, having, perhaps, enjoyed the supreme satisfaction of taking part in a real raid—*

WHO WOULD PREFER, *TO THESE EXCITEMENTS,*
A SEDATE AND LEGAL DINNER,
EVEN *if the* WINES **OF** THE WORLD
WERE *at his* **DISPOSAL?**

—*Lucy Moore,* ANYTHING GOES

SPEAKEASY: *The Underground Social Scene*

Hiding in plain sight behind storefronts, basement doors, and other creative facades—with entry permitted only by way of passwords, specific handshakes, or secret knocks—speakeasies popped up all over the United States in the early 1920s, after the ratification of the 18th Amendment, banning the manufacture, sale, and transportation of alcoholic beverages. In case of a raid, many speakeasies served cocktails in teacups, installed elaborate alarms, and stashed the contraband liquor in secret cabinets and other clever hiding places.

Social barriers were broken, as women entered the bar scene, and rich and poor alike conspired together to drink and avoid the law. African American musicians, too, mingled and found work in the underground clubs, as jazz became mainstream and dancing took off as the new social craze.

As America banned the booze, London celebrated the end of the Great War in style. In 1921, the wartime Licensing Act was finally altered to allow drink to be served until 12:30 a.m., as long as it was accompanied by food. When the cocktail parties at swish Mayfair houses got "too tired-making," the Bright Young People headed to their favorite London nightclubs, which usually began filling up around 11:30 p.m. There the restless young souls could round off the evening doing the Charleston, Shimmy, and Heebie Jeebie to the thrilling sounds of the house jazz band.

The Gargoyle Club

The Bright Young People, as ever, weren't averse to making their own fun when it came to the dashing nightclub scene. When he wanted somewhere new to dance with his girlfriend, David Tennant, the son of Lord Glenconner and one of the leading members of the Bright Young People, took matters into his own hands and opened the Gargoyle Club on Dean Street in London. The venue promised a fashionable dance hall with an artistic bent, where "struggling writers, painters, poets and musicians will be offered the best food and wine at prices they can afford."

On the advice of his friend Henri Matisse, David lined the walls with shards of broken mirrors and hung the artist's paintings. Membership was seven guineas ($556 today) but free to the "deserving artistic poor," as the atmosphere was decidedly bohe-

100

MAKING MERRY WITH MEYRICK

Club owner Kate Meyrick became a celebrity in London circles—before becoming infamous for her many arrests and spells in jail. On a typical evening at her 43 Club you could find foreign royalty, such as the King of Sweden, sharing the dance floor with stars like Tallulah Bankhead, various peers of the realm, and theatre impresario Jimmy White, as well as the occasional London gangster or murderer.

Mrs. Meyrick herself became very well connected; two of her daughters married members of the peerage, while a third would go on to marry a lord.

mian. Daphne Fielding remarked that "the Gargoyle seemed to transform ordinary conventional people into bohemians; on becoming members they even began to dress quite differently."

The Lido

In France, the place to be was undoubtedly the decadent Lido on the Champs Élysées, at the heart of elegant Paris. A heady mixture of a swimming pool, restaurant, cabaret, and club, it was inspired by the success of the Venetian Lido and billed as the most luxurious venue in all of Europe. It opened on February 18,

1928, amid a fanfare of hyperbole—but it lived up to its promise. A block long, the Lido was entered via elevator, which descended to the basement to what revelers described as a "magical underworld." Here the pink-and-blue marbled pool took center stage, with a lavish bar at one end, grand marble pillars surrounding its edge, and multicolored lights setting a dreamy scene. The pool's water was lightly scented with hyacinth.

The Ritz Bar

The Ritz Bar in Paris was one venue where the great and the glittering could always be found. A favorite haunt of Cole Porter and Noël Coward—who named a play that never saw the light of day after the bar—the venue was split into two, with a men-only bar and a mixed bar.

In *The Sweet and Twenties,* Beverley Nichols wrote, "I adored the Ritz Bar. Think of it . . . champagne cocktails at a bob apiece! And the scent of Gauloise cigarettes, and the echo of Madame Chanel's laughter . . . and the sudden flurry of [cabaret star] Mistinguett, wrapped to the hilt in monkey fur, stepping over the sacred masculine threshold in pursuit of her latest young man, who is drinking behind a pillar with a rather dubious Jamaican."

Cabaret had been born in 1881 at Le Chat Noir (The Black Cat) in Montmartre, Paris. By the 1920s, the format not only had spread all over Europe, with cabaret clubs in London, Berlin, and Amsterdam, but had produced many more infamous venues in Paris itself, too. With hot jazz tunes, newfangled choreography, and potent cocktails fueling the fun, nights out had never been so entertaining.

The Moulin Rouge

With its iconic windmill on the roof, the Moulin Rouge was destroyed by fire in 1915 but reopened in 1921 with a huge new show. Mistinguett, a beautiful French singer and actress—and the highest-paid female entertainer of the time—headlined the sold-out revues, which often featured her younger lover, Maurice Chevalier.

In 1918, the Folies Bergère had been taken over by Paul Derval, who introduced more extravagant costumes and special effects, as well as the "small nude women" who would become the venue's trademark as its success grew throughout the twenties. The shows often reflected the Parisian fascination with the black immigrants who now lived in the city. It was here, in 1926, that Josephine Baker became an overnight sensation with her *Danse Sauvage*, wearing a skirt made of a string of artificial bananas and little else.

The Ziegfeld Follies

Among the hopefuls who were turned down by Florenz Ziegfeld before going on to make it big elsewhere were Norma Shearer, Joan Crawford, Gypsy Rose Lee, Lucille Ball, and Hedda Hopper.

One of the most daring shows in New York was *The Ziegfeld Follies* at Broadway's New Amsterdam Theatre. Based on the famous Folies Bergère in Paris, the show was started in 1907 by impresario Florenz Ziegfeld and featured vaudeville acts, comedians, singers, and most importantly, scantily clad chorus girls. In the early twenties, the *Follies* was more popular than ever and the famous names to appear in the show included W. C. Fields and Fanny Brice. Showgirls, including future stars Barbara Stanwyck and Paulette Goddard, as well as flapper extraordinaire Louise Brooks, were handpicked for their beauty and grace by notorious womanizer Ziegfeld, who enjoyed affairs with many of his protégées. They paraded on stage in a variety of costumes by top designers of the day and drew huge crowds, often leaving the show to marry wealthy admirers.

The annual Ziegfeld Ball, where many of the dancing girls met future husbands, continued as a social event of the season for years after the last production of the *Follies* in 1931.

Cabaret in the UK

Many of the 1920s London nightclubs provided more than a tipple and a chance to dance, too. Musical entertainment was often laid on in the form of a cabaret, with dancing girls, musicians, and singers. The trade in the UK clubs was given a boost by a 1923 law that banned bars at the old-fashioned music halls, meaning that those who could afford it, and wanted a drink with their evening's entertainment, deserted the traditional venues. Nightclub owners paid a premium for entertainers with a following who could attract the crowds.

The Kit Cat Club

The Kit Cat Club opened in 1925 in Haymarket, London, and was billed as "luxurious, but wonderfully comfy . . . a vastly patronized and fashionable resort." Its membership soon exceeded six thousand, and included princes, cabinet ministers, dukes, and peers.

As well as restaurants, bars, and a huge dance floor, the club boasted the best cabaret in town, sharing acts with the nearby Piccadilly Hotel, which was owned by the same syndicate of investors. The headliners for the grand opening were the famous American entertainers the Dolly Sisters, who were shortly to appear at the famous Moulin Rouge in Paris. But in December 1926, a year after it opened, the club was raided and the proprietors were fined £500 (more than $36,600 today) each, plus £156 (more than $11,000) costs, for serving drinks after hours.

The venue reopened as a restaurant under new management in May 1927, but still boasted a glittering cabaret, including the internationally renowned dancer and comedian Johnny Hudgins—known as the Wah Wah Man because of his comedy mime act, which was always accompanied by sound effects from a muted jazz trumpet—and American singer and comedienne Sophie Tucker.

CABARET NIGHT FOR THE MODERN FLAPPER

The art of the cabaret has survived and has been refreshed for the new millennium. Check out these clubs for special cabaret nights (ranging from standard live jazz to scantily-clad ensemble performances) the next time you're in New York City:

CAFÉ CARLYLE
981 Madison Avenue
rosewoodhotels.com/en
/carlyle/dining/cafe_carlyle

DON'T TELL MAMA
343 West 46th Street
donttellmamanyc.com
/cabaret.php

**THE DUPLEX PIANO BAR
& CABARET**
61 Christopher Street
theduplex.com/cabaret
/dct.shtml

LE SCANDAL CABARET
407 West 42nd Street
lescandal.com

METROPOLITAN ROOM
34 West 22nd Street
metropolitanroom.com/index.cfm

ROSELAND BALLROOM
239 West 52nd Street
roselandballroom.com

THE RUM HOUSE
228 West 47th Street
edisonrumhouse.com

ZEBULON CAFÉ CONCERT
258 Wythe Avenue
Brooklyn
zebuloncafeconcert.com

ZINC BAR
82 West 3rd Street
zincbar.com

What does it mean to have "star power"? In the music world, it's all about doing (or being) something new, and these four stars epitomize the music star scene of the Roaring '20s. It's never too late to be a protégé . . .

Lillian Lorraine

Discovered by dance impresario Florenz Ziegfeld in 1907, at the age of fifteen, Lillian Lorraine became one of his biggest stars in the 1910s, and was still drawing crowds in the 1920s. Her many high-profile love affairs, including with Ziegfeld himself, regularly filled newspaper columns and her many marriages proved short-lived. Her star faded toward the end of the decade and she moved on to vaudeville.

In *Scandals and Follies*, his biography of Ziegfeld, author Lee Davis wrote: "[Ziegfeld] was insanely in love with Lillian Lorraine and would remain so, to one degree or another, for the rest of his life, despite her erratic, irresponsible, often senseless behavior, her multiple marriages to other men, his own two marriages and his need for all his adult life to sleep with the best of the beauties he hired."

Josephine Baker

Born in Missouri, Josephine Baker was introduced to vaudeville after she was spotted dancing for money on street corners at the age of fifteen. After a spell in Harlem, she moved to Paris to star at the Folies Bergère, causing a stir with her sensual dancing, comedic talent, uninhibited routines, and barely-there costumes. She was the first African American woman to become an international entertainer, and was showered with gifts from admirers, including motorcars, precious gems, and more than 1,500 marriage proposals. She went on to become a leading supporter of the civil rights movement in the United States, and an active member of the French Resistance during the Second World War. She also raised twelve adopted children from various ethnic backgrounds.

Duke Ellington

Born Edward Kennedy Ellington in Washington, DC, the Duke moved to Harlem, the hub of the jazz revolution, in the early twenties. In 1923, jazz musician Elmer Snowden led the house band at New York's Hollywood Club, which Ellington took over as band leader a year later. The Duke went on to a residency at Harlem's famous Cotton Club and a lucrative broadcasting career. He also recorded hundreds of hit records, including "It Don't Mean a Thing (If It Ain't Got That Swing)." He is famous for spreading the popularity of jazz music and elevating it to an art form. He also composed over a thousand songs in a career that spanned more than fifty years.

In his book *The Swing Era,* musician Gunther Schuller wrote: "Music was indeed [Duke Ellington's] mistress; it was his total life and his commitment to it was incomparable and unalterable.

In jazz he was a giant among giants. And in twentieth-century music, he may yet one day be recognized as one of the half-dozen greatest masters of our time."

Louis Armstrong

Born in 1901 in Louisiana, Louis Armstrong moved to Chicago at the age of twenty-one to play the trumpet in Joe "King" Oliver's Creole Jazz Band, and later joined the highly respected Fletcher Henderson Orchestra in New York. In 1924 he recorded with contemporary jazz singers including Bessie Smith, Ma Rainey, and Alberta Hunter. In 1925, he formed Louis Armstrong and the Hot Five (sometimes the Hot Seven), and their 1928 recording of "West End Blues," including a legendary trumpet intro from Louis, is considered a masterpiece of the Jazz Age. He soon moved into vocals, and his version of "Ain't Misbehavin'" was one of the biggest hits of the decade.

Asked to define jazz, Louis reportedly answered, "If you have to ask what jazz is, you'll never know."

ENTERTAIN YOURSELF

For the fun-loving set, the Jazz Age was the perfect era in which to be living life to the fullest. Just as modern inventions were revolutionizing home life, the march of progress was also making itself felt in the world of show business, with radio and cinema leading the way with exciting innovations, and stagecraft becoming ever more entertaining.

IF YOU CAN DREAM IT, YOU CAN DO IT.

—*Walt Disney*

RADIO SETS IN THE HOME

Although Marconi had patented the first radio in 1896, transmission was banned in most countries between 1914 and 1918 and the "wireless" didn't take off until well after the First World War. But throughout the twenties its growth worldwide was phenomenal. In the United States, for example, between 1923 and 1930, 60 percent of families bought radio sets. By 1928, the United States boasted three national radio networks: two from the National Broadcasting Company (NBC) and one from the Columbia Broadcasting System (CBS).

The concept of home entertainment was born toward the end of the decade, as live music recordings, news reports, commentary, comedies, and fictional stories could be enjoyed in the comfort of the living room.

TINSELTOWN:
The First Hollywood Studios and the Silent Silver Screen

The first Hollywood studio, Nestor, had cranked up its cameras in 1911 and by the dawn of the Jazz Age decade, the Los Angeles suburb had established itself as the hub of the film industry, the "dream factory." Major studios run by Warner Bros., Samuel Goldwyn, Louis B. Mayer, and William Fox had sprung up, as well as Universal Studios and comedy specialists Keystone, producers of the "Keystone Cops" series.

The Silent Silver Screen

After the drab, depressing days of the war, people craved laughter and glamour—and Hollywood had plenty to give. Stars like Gloria Swanson, Norma Shearer, Louise Brooks, Clara Bow, and Mary Pickford had young audiences sighing with admiration, and leading men Rudolph Valentino and Douglas Fairbanks quickened the pulse of many a girl with romance on her mind. Slapstick comedies had the filmgoers flocking to the picture houses by the thousands. But never a word was spoken. The twenties was the golden age of the silent movie.

The following movies capture the glamour of early Hollywood and the vision of innovative directors of the era:

The Cabinet of Dr. Caligari (drama, 1920)

The Kid (comedy, 1921)

The Four Horsemen of the Apocalypse (action/adventure, 1921)

Nanook of the North (documentary, 1922)

The Hunchback of Notre Dame (drama, 1923)

Greed (drama, 1924)

The Phantom of the Opera (drama, 1925)

It (romantic comedy, 1927)

My Best Girl (romantic comedy, 1927)

Pandora's Box (drama, 1929)

Silent slapstick was big business for the studios, and Charlie Chaplin, Harold Lloyd, and Buster Keaton were the kings of comedy. London-born Chaplin brought moviegoers flocking with movies such as *The Kid* (1921) and *The Gold Rush* (1923), while Keaton—known as the Great Stone Face—set up his own production company in 1921 and starred in silent classics such as *The General* (1926) and *The Cameraman* (1928). Harold Lloyd had played luckless down-and-outs in short films before the twenties but, having created the new persona of a fearless young man capable of anything—with the simple aid of a pair of black-rimmed glasses—he moved into feature films in 1921 with the successful *Sailor-Made Man* (1921) and *Grandma's Boy* (1922). A year later came *Safety Last*, which included the classic scene of Lloyd clinging from the hands of a clock at the top of a sky-scraper he had just climbed. By the mid-twenties he was earning around $1.5 million—the equivalent of $18.7 million today.

ADDING SOUND TO MOVIES
WOULD BE LIKE PUTTING LIPSTICK ON THE
VENUS ⬩ᴅᴇ⬩ MILO.

—Mary Pickford, film actress

HOST A '20s MOVIE NIGHT

Play three of the following films for a '20s Movie Night. Make your favorite Prohibition cocktail and be prepared for some roaring entertainment!

COMEDY: *The Haunted House* (1921)
Cops (1922)
Safety Last (1923)
The Gold Rush (1925)
The Circus (1928)

DRAMA: *Isn't Life Wonderful* (1924)
The Jazz Singer (1927)
Flesh and the Devil (1927)
The Last Command (1928)
The Passion of Joan of Arc (1928)

ACTION: *The Last of the Mohicans* (1920)
The Three Musketeers (1921)
Robin Hood (1922)
The Gaucho (1927)
Metropolis (1927)

In the years leading up to the twenties, actress Theda Bara had made the vamp look fashionable, with the skimpy clothing, the black-rimmed eyes, and the blood red lips of costume dramas such as *Cleopatra* and *Salome*. Gloria Swanson carried on the tradition in such movies as *Sadie Thompson* (1928) and *Queen Kelly* (1929), produced by her lover, Joseph Kennedy, the father of future president John F. Kennedy. Toward the end of the decade, Greta Garbo added her smoldering good looks to the movie billboards, playing the femme fatale in both silent and talking films.

The First Film Flapper: Olive Thomas

Clara Bow, Louise Brooks, and Joan Crawford all personified the flapper on screen, but the first actress to claim the title lived the life both on and off the screen, and all too briefly. In 1920, Olive Thomas starred as a rebellious schoolgirl in *The Flapper*. The wild actress was reveling in the party lifestyle long before the Roaring Twenties, with husband Jack Pickford, brother of screen icon Mary Pickford. Thomas and Pickford were renowned for their drink and drugs binges, and the twenty-six-year-old actress died in a hotel room shortly after *The Flapper* was released, when she accidentally drank mercury bichloride solution, prescribed as an external ointment for Jack's syphilis.

The First Action Star: Rudolph Valentino

Whenever he was in London, another leading Hollywood star, Rudolph Valentino, made a beeline for the 43 Club, where "his svelte figure and fascinating face used to immediately attract the attention of everyone in the place." In *Secrets of the 43 Club*,

Kate Meyrick recalled a meeting between the actor and a young peeress, which she overheard from behind a screen where she was working:

"It was perfectly obvious that the young woman was wildly in love with Valentino, and it was equally evident that he did not reciprocate her passion. She behaved like a silly girl, trying to draw him out on the subject of love and telling tedious stories about the marriage proposals she claimed to have received. . . . It was painful to listen to her making such a fool of herself. . . . A few nights later I heard this same peeress give her impression of Valentino. 'He's quite a decent young kid,' she said. 'But he hasn't got any particular depth of character.' "

THE JAZZ SINGER: *Enter, The Talkie*

The Jazz Singer premiered on October 6, 1927, and sounded the death toll for silent movies. Al Jolson starred as a would-be jazz artist forced to defy his family to achieve his dream, and for the first time, an actor moved his lips as spoken dialogue was heard. The first words Jolson spoke were, "Wait a minute, wait a minute, you ain't heard nothin' yet! Wait a minute, I tell ya! You ain't heard nothin'!"

Doris Warner, the daughter of Warner Bros. studio founder Harry, was at the New York screening and remembered that at these prophetic words "the audience became hysterical." Critic Robert E. Sherwood, who reviewed the film, later said the dialogue scene between Jolson and costar Eugenie Besserer was "fraught with tremendous significance . . . I for one suddenly realized that the end of the silent drama is in sight."

The first full-length talkie was a huge hit, taking $2.6 million at the box office ($32 million today). Sadly none of the Warner brothers were there to see the film premiere—Sam Warner died the day before the screening and his three brothers, Harry, Albert, and Jack, had returned to California for his funeral.

Now that Al Jolson had spoken, the public was eager to hear the dulcet tones of their screen idols. But not all fared well in the talkies revolution. Studios introduced voice tests and many actors and actresses saw their contracts renegotiated or terminated. Louise Brooks, for example, walked out when her studio attempted to reduce her salary.

IF I WERE AN ACTOR WITH A SQUEAKY VOICE,

I WOULD WORRY.

—*Welford Beaton, cinema critic, on the release of* THE JAZZ SINGER

Accents were often a stumbling block, especially for the careers of action star Rudolph Valentino's beautiful lover, Polish actress Pola Negri, and Mexican actor Ramón Novarro. Others, like John Gilbert and Douglas Fairbanks, found the parts drying up because their voices didn't match their screen personas. Clara Bow, whose image defined the twenties Jazz Age, was out of work because her thick Brooklyn accent didn't suit the celluloid. Greta Garbo, Joan Crawford, Lon Chaney, and Gloria Swanson were among the stars who made the transition to talkies and continued to enjoy huge Hollywood success.

The 1928 animated feature *Steamboat Willie* saw the birth of a movie legend—Mickey Mouse. Inspired by a pet mouse on Walt Disney's farm, he was called Mortimer until Walt's wife, Lillian, persuaded Walt to change the name. The cute little character and his beloved Minnie, both voiced by their creator, were an instant success and went on to star in many more cartoons, as the Disney empire grew from a tiny animation studio into a multi-million-dollar Hollywood giant. In years to come, Walt Disney would comment, "I only hope that we never lose sight of one thing—that it was all started by a mouse."

WE FELT THAT THE PUBLIC,

and especially the children, like animals that are cute and little. I think we are rather INDEBTED to Charlie Chaplin for the idea. We wanted something appealing, and we thought of

A TINY BIT ☝ A MOUSE

that would have something of the wistfulness of Chaplin ▶▶▶

A LITTLE FELLOW

TRYING TO DO THE BEST HE COULD.

—*Walt Disney, quoted in* DISNEY AND HIS WORLDS *by Alan Bryman*

Do you dream of the big screen? The 1920s was one of the most interesting decades in the film world, and these three actors were some of the first movie stars in America.

Charlie Chaplin

Having grown up in poverty in London, Charles Chaplin moved to Hollywood at the age of twenty-four and was hired by Keystone. After borrowing Fatty Arbuckle's trousers and a derby hat, he invented the slapstick character of the Little Tramp, who debuted in the 1914 movie *Kid Auto Races at Venice.* In 1919, he formed United Artists with Mary Pickford, Douglas Fairbanks, and D. W. Griffith. He enjoyed huge success throughout the twenties and even survived the advent of the talkies. He appeared in box office hits including *The Kid, The Gold Rush,* and *The Great Dictator,* and wrote the classic song "Smile." The first time the voice of the Tramp was heard was at the end of the 1936 movie *Modern Times*.

Chaplin's movie career came to an abrupt halt in 1952 when, targeted by Senator Joseph McCarthy's anticommunist witch hunt, he left the United States and settled in Switzerland.

Greta Garbo

Signed up by Louis B. Mayer in 1925, Greta Garbo moved to the United States from her native Sweden and made her first Hollywood movie, *The Torrent,* in 1925. In 1927, she made *Flesh and the Devil* and the chemistry with costar John Gilbert, both on and off screen, made her the talk of Tinseltown and darling of the gossip columns. As the talkies arrived, Greta took lessons to modify her Swedish accent, and her husky, seductive tones made her a hit with audiences all over again. She retired from the screen in 1941 and lived a reclusive life until her death in 1990.

Mary Pickford

Besides Charlie Chaplin, Mary Pickford was the biggest box office star of the 1920s. Referred to as "Little Mary" and "America's Sweetheart," she played everything from young innocent girls to prostitutes—and always for a handsome salary. By 1918, Mary was earning $10,000 a week—the equivalent of over $150,000 today—but she declared that was not enough and moved to First National Studios for $675,000 (over $10 million today). By 1922 she was Hollywood's first millionaire star. After setting up United Artists with Charlie Chaplin, D. W. Griffith, and her future husband Douglas Fairbanks, Mary starred in some of the biggest movies of the silent era, including *Pollyanna* (1920), *Rosita* (1923), and *Little Lord Fauntleroy* (1921), in which she played both the little boy and his widowed mother.

SOURCES AND BIBLIOGRAPHY

BOOKS

Cally Blackman, *Fashion of the Twenties and Thirties* (Heinemann Books)

Barbara Cartland, *We Danced All Night* (Hutchinson)

Jan Dalley, *Diana Mosley* (Faber and Faber)

Frank Dawes, *Not in Front of the Servants* (Hutchinson)

F. Scott Fitzgerald, *The Great Gatsby* (Wordsworth Classics)

Jackie Gaff, *20th Century Design: Twenties and Thirties* (Heinemann Books)

Selena Hastings, *Nancy Mitford* (Vintage Books)

Pamela Horn, *Life Below Stairs in the 20th Century* (Sutton Publishing)

Michael Horsham, *20s and 30s Style* (Grange Books)

The Hulton Getty Picture Library, *The 1920s* (Konemann)

Marie-Jaqueline Lancaster, *Brian Howard: Portrait of a Failure* (Green Candy Press)

Loelia Lindsay, *Grace and Favour: The Memoirs of Loelia, Duchess of Westminster* (Weidenfeld & Nicolson)

Mary S. Lovell, *The Mitford Girls* (Abacus)

Kate Meyrick, *Secrets of the 43 Club* (Parkgate Publishing)

Marie Therese Miller-Degenfeld, *Memoirs of Marie Therese Miller-Degenfeld* (Trafford Publishing)

Lucy Moore, *Anything Goes* (Atlantic Books)

Beverley Nichols, *The Sweet and Twenties* (Weidenfeld & Nicolson)

Steve Parker, *20th Century Media: Twenties and Thirties* (Heinemann Books)

Margaret Powell, *Below Stairs* (Pan Books)

Martin Pugh, *We Danced All Night* (Vintage Books)

Peter Sussman (ed.), *Decca: The Letters of Jessica Mitford* (Weidenfeld & Nicolson)

Richard Tames, *Picture History of the 20th Century: The 1920s* (Franklin Watts)

D. J. Taylor, *Bright Young People* (Vintage Books)

Evelyn Waugh, *Brideshead Revisited* (Penguin)

Evelyn Waugh, *Vile Bodies* (Marshall Cavendish)

WEBSITES

www.1920-30.com
www.aohg.org.uk/twww
www.dailymail.co.uk
www.fotolibra.com
www.havemann.com
www.headoverheelshistory.com
www.independent.co.uk
www.jazzageclub.com
www.jazzbabies.com
www.measuringworth.com
www.nytimes.com
www.proquestk12.com
www.telegraph.co.uk
www.thepeoplehistory.com
www.thetimes.co.uk
www.thisisstafford.co.uk

bookflaps.blogspot.com/2011
   /04/flappers-dictionary.html
www.ultimatehistoryproject.com
   /flapper.html
www.moderndayflapper.com
www.artdecosociety.org
www.legendsofamerica.com
kcts9.org/prohibition/flapper
   -slang-talk-1920s-talk
www.vintagegown.com/history
   /history_1920a.htm
www.pbs.org/kteh/amstory
   tellers/bios.html
www.ehow.com/info_8291791
   _bar-drinks-roaring-20s.html

GATSBY

BELIEVED IN THE GREEN LIGHT,
🎟 ORGIASTIC FUTURE
that year by year recedes before us.

‹‹‹‹‹‹‹‹‹‹‹‹‹‹ ◄◆► ››››››››››››››››

IT ELUDED US THEN,

BUT THAT'S NO MATTER ◄◆►

TOMORROW

we will run faster, stretch out our arms farther …
AND ONE FINE MORNING ◄◆►

‹‹‹‹‹‹‹‹‹‹‹‹‹‹ ◄◆► ››››››››››››››››

SO WE BEAT ON,

BOATS AGAINST THE CURRENT,

BORNE BACK CEASELESSLY INTO THE PAST.

—*F. Scott Fitzgerald,* THE GREAT GATSBY